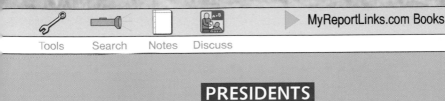
PRESIDENTS

GEORGE H. W. BUSH

A MyReportLinks.com Book

Tim O'Shei & Joe Marren

MyReportLinks.com Books

an imprint of

Enslow Publishers, Inc.

Box 398, 40 Industrial Road
Berkeley Heights, NJ 07922
USA

MyReportLinks.com Books, an imprint of Enslow Publishers, Inc. MyReportLinks is a trademark of Enslow Publishers, Inc.

Library of Congress Cataloging-in-Publication Data

O'Shei, Tim.
George H.W. Bush / Tim O'Shei & Joe Marren.
    p. cm. — (Presidents)
Summary: A biography of George Bush, who served as Vice President under Ronald Reagan and led the country during the 1991 Persian Gulf War. Includes Internet links to Web sites, source documents, and photographs related to George Herbert Walker Bush.
Includes bibliographical references and index.
ISBN 0-7660-5132-3
1. Bush, George, 1924—Juvenile literature. 2. Presidents—United States—Biography—Juvenile literature. [1. Bush, George, 1924– 2. Presidents.]
I. Marren, Joe. II. Title. III. Series.
E903.O838 2003
973.931'092—dc21

2003011184

20857

Printed in the United States of America

10 9 8 7 6 5 4 3 2 1

To Our Readers:
Through the purchase of this book, you and your library gain access to the Report Links that specifically back up this book.
The Publisher will provide access to the Report Links that back up this book and will keep these Report Links up to date on **www.myreportlinks.com** for three years from the book's first publication date.
We have done our best to make sure all Internet addresses in this book were active and appropriate when we went to press. However, the author and the Publisher have no control over, and assume no liability for, the material available on those Internet sites or on other Web sites they may link to.
The usage of the MyReportLinks.com Books Web site is subject to the terms and conditions stated on the Usage Policy Statement on **www.myreportlinks.com**.
A password may be required to access the Report Links that back up this book. The password is found on the bottom of page 4 of this book.
Any comments or suggestions can be sent by e-mail to comments@myreportlinks.com or to the address on the back cover.

Contents

MyReportLinks.com Books
Great Books, Great Links, Great for Research!

MyReportLinks.com Books present the information you need to learn about your report subject. In addition, they show you where to go on the Internet for more information. The pre-evaluated Report Links that back up this book are kept up to date on **www.myreportlinks.com**. With the purchase of a MyReportLinks.com Books title, you and your library gain access to the Report Links that specifically back up that book. The Report Links save hours of research time and link to dozens—even hundreds—of Web sites, source documents, and photos related to your report topic.

Please see "To Our Readers" on the Copyright page for important information about this book, the MyReportLinks.com Books Web site, and the Report Links that back up this book.

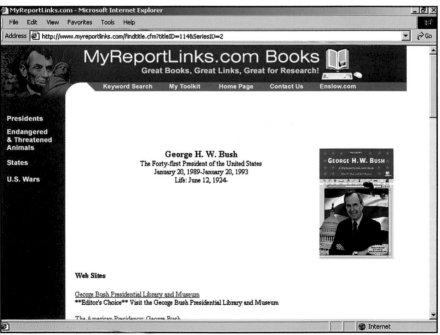

Access:

The Publisher will provide access to the Report Links that back up this book and will try to keep these Report Links up to date on our Web site for three years from the book's first publication date. Please enter **PGB7262** if asked for a password.

Report Links

The Internet sites described below can be accessed at
http://www.myreportlinks.com

*EDITOR'S CHOICE

▶**George Bush Presidential Library and Museum**
The George Bush Presidential Library and Museum holds the
biographies of George and Barbara Bush. You can also take a virtual
tour of the museum, view photos, and learn about exhibits at the
museum. Click on "Research" to read public papers.

Link to this Internet site from http://www.myreportlinks.com

*EDITOR'S CHOICE

▶**The American Presidency: George Bush**
The American Presidency Web site provides a brief biography of
George Bush. Here you will learn about his early political career, vice
presidency, and rise to the presidency. You will also learn about the
Persian Gulf War.

Link to this Internet site from http://www.myreportlinks.com

*EDITOR'S CHOICE

▶**"I Do Solemnly Swear . . ." George Bush**
At this Library of Congress Web site you can experience George H. W. Bush's
inauguration day through images and documents, including the text to
Bush's inaugural address.

Link to this Internet site from http://www.myreportlinks.com

*EDITOR'S CHOICE

▶**The Gulf War**
At this PBS Web site you will find oral histories and war stories, and
you can learn about weapons and technology used during the Gulf
War. You will also find maps and a chronology of events.

Link to this Internet site from http://www.myreportlinks.com

*EDITOR'S CHOICE

▶**The White House: George Bush**
The official White House Web site holds the biography of George
Bush. Here you will learn about his early years, vice presidency,
and presidency.

Link to this Internet site from http://www.myreportlinks.com

*EDITOR'S CHOICE

▶**George Herbert Walker Bush (1989–1993)**
At the American President Web site you can explore the presidency
of George Herbert Walker Bush. Here you will find a comprehensive
biography of Bush and First Lady Barbara Bush. You will also learn
about his cabinet members, staff advisors, and key players.

Link to this Internet site from http://www.myreportlinks.com

Report Links

The Internet sites described below can be accessed at
http://www.myreportlinks.com

▶**The American Presidency: Iran-Contra Affair**
At the American Presidency Web site you will find a brief description of the
Iran-Contra Affair, which occurred while Bush was serving as vice president to
Ronald Reagan.

Link to this Internet site from http://www.myreportlinks.com

▶**The American Presidency: James Danforth Quayle**
Here you will find a brief biography of Vice President Dan Quayle. You will
learn about his experiences as vice president under George H.W. Bush, as well
as other highlights of his political career.

Link to this Internet site from http://www.myreportlinks.com

▶**American Presidents: Life Portraits: George Bush**
The American Presidents Web site provides essential information about
George Bush. Here you will find "Life Facts" and "Did you know?" trivia.
You can also read Bush's comments to children who attended a Halloween
party at the White House.

Link to this Internet site from http://www.myreportlinks.com

▶*Character Above All:* **George Bush**
At this PBS Web site you will find an essay about George Bush from the book
of essays entitled *Character Above All.* This essay discusses how Bush handled
his three campaigns for president as well as his presidency.

Link to this Internet site from http://www.myreportlinks.com

▶**Fact Monster: George Herbert Walker Bush**
Fact Monster provides a brief introduction to George H.W. Bush.
Here you will learn about his early life, college years, and political
career, including his presidency.

Link to this Internet site from http://www.myreportlinks.com

▶**George H.W. Bush: Iraqi Aggression in the Persian Gulf**
Read George H.W. Bush's speech justifying the aims of the United States
during the Persian Gulf War.

Link to this Internet site from http://www.myreportlinks.com

Report Links

▶ **George Herbert Walker Bush**
At the CNN Interactive Cold War Web site you can read a brief profile of George Herbert Walker Bush and his experiences in the Cold War while he was vice president under Ronald Reagan.

Link to this Internet site from http://www.myreportlinks.com

▶ **George Herbert Walker Bush**
The POTUS Web site provides general facts about George Bush's family, education, and government positions. You will also find election results and a list of Bush's cabinet members.

Link to this Internet site from http://www.myreportlinks.com

▶ **George Herbert Walker Bush (1924–)**
This Web site holds the text to speeches made by George H.W. Bush. Here you will find his inaugural address and his 1990, 1991, and 1992 State of the Union addresses.

Link to this Internet site from http://www.myreportlinks.com

▶ **The Hall of Public Service: George Bush**
In 1995, George Bush was inducted into the Academy of Achievement. At this Web site you will find a brief profile of George Bush, his biography, and an interview with the former president.

Link to this Internet site from http://www.myreportlinks.com

▶ **Lieutenant Junior Grade George Bush, USNR**
At the Naval Historic Center Web site you can read about George H.W. Bush's naval career. Here you will learn about Bush's experiences in World War II and the decorations he received.

Link to this Internet site from http://www.myreportlinks.com

▶ **The Living Room Candidate: 1988**
In 1988, George H.W. Bush ran for president against Michael Dukakis. At the Living Room Candidate Web site you can explore the campaign issues and learn how television was used to express their points of view.

Link to this Internet site from http://www.myreportlinks.com

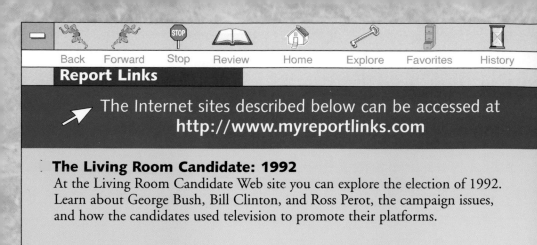

Back	Forward	Stop	Review	Home	Explore	Favorites	History

Report Links

➤ The Internet sites described below can be accessed at
http://www.myreportlinks.com

The Living Room Candidate: 1992

At the Living Room Candidate Web site you can explore the election of 1992. Learn about George Bush, Bill Clinton, and Ross Perot, the campaign issues, and how the candidates used television to promote their platforms.

Link to this Internet site from http://www.myreportlinks.com

The Long Road to War

The Long Road to War explores the history of the United States' relationship with Iraq since 1990. Here you will find several online companions to documentaries from *Frontline*, which include an interview, chronologies, and commentary.

Link to this Internet site from http://www.myreportlinks.com

Mr. President: George Bush

This Smithsonian Web site provides a profile of George H.W. Bush. Here you will find a quote, "fast facts," and a brief description highlighting Bush's military experience.

Link to this Internet site from http://www.myreportlinks.com

Objects from the Presidency

At this Web site you can explore the objects and era of George H.W. Bush's presidency as well as those of other United States presidents. You will also find a brief description of Bush's administration.

Link to this Internet site from http://www.myreportlinks.com

Panama Canal Handover

This CNN Web site explores the history of the Panama Canal. Here you will learn about the events that led up to the 1989 Panama Invasion that took place under George H.W. Bush.

Link to this Internet site from http://www.myreportlinks.com

Presidential Visits Abroad

From the State Department Web site you can view a listing of George H.W. Bush's trips abroad from January 20, 1989, through January 20, 1993.

Link to this Internet site from http://www.myreportlinks.com

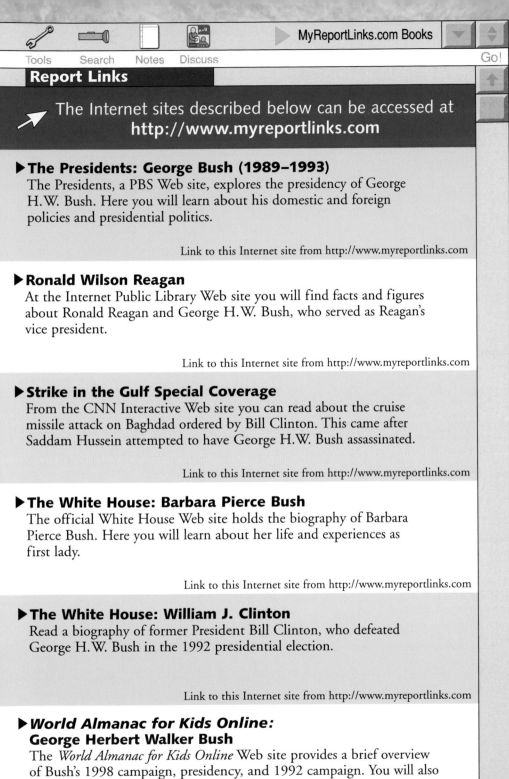
Report Links

The Internet sites described below can be accessed at
http://www.myreportlinks.com

▶ **The Presidents: George Bush (1989–1993)**
The Presidents, a PBS Web site, explores the presidency of George
H.W. Bush. Here you will learn about his domestic and foreign
policies and presidential politics.

Link to this Internet site from http://www.myreportlinks.com

▶ **Ronald Wilson Reagan**
At the Internet Public Library Web site you will find facts and figures
about Ronald Reagan and George H.W. Bush, who served as Reagan's
vice president.

Link to this Internet site from http://www.myreportlinks.com

▶ **Strike in the Gulf Special Coverage**
From the CNN Interactive Web site you can read about the cruise
missile attack on Baghdad ordered by Bill Clinton. This came after
Saddam Hussein attempted to have George H.W. Bush assassinated.

Link to this Internet site from http://www.myreportlinks.com

▶ **The White House: Barbara Pierce Bush**
The official White House Web site holds the biography of Barbara
Pierce Bush. Here you will learn about her life and experiences as
first lady.

Link to this Internet site from http://www.myreportlinks.com

▶ **The White House: William J. Clinton**
Read a biography of former President Bill Clinton, who defeated
George H.W. Bush in the 1992 presidential election.

Link to this Internet site from http://www.myreportlinks.com

▶ *World Almanac for Kids Online:*
George Herbert Walker Bush
The *World Almanac for Kids Online* Web site provides a brief overview
of Bush's 1998 campaign, presidency, and 1992 campaign. You will also
learn about his life after leaving the White House.

Link to this Internet site from http://www.myreportlinks.com

1924—*June 12:* Born in Milton, Massachusetts. The family moves to Greenwich, Connecticut, shortly thereafter.

1937—Enrolls in Phillips Academy.

1942—*June 12:* Joins the U.S. Navy and becomes the youngest fighter pilot in the fleet.

1944—*Sept. 2:* His plane is shot down and he bails out over the Pacific Ocean during World War II.

1945—*Jan. 6:* Marries Barbara Pierce.

—Enrolls in Yale University.

1946—*July 6:* His son, George W. Bush, is born.

1948—Graduates from Yale.

—Moves to Texas to take a job in the oil and gas industry.

1950—Quits his job and forms Bush-Overbey Oil Development Company.

1952—His father, Prescott Bush, is elected senator from Connecticut.

1953—*Feb. 11:* His son, Jeb, is born.

—*Oct. 11:* His daughter, Robin, dies of leukemia.

—Forms a new company, Zapata Petroleum Corporation.

1954—He and his partners form the Zapata Off-Shore Company; Bush is its president.

1955—*Jan. 22:* His son, Neil M. Bush, is born.

1956—*Oct. 22:* His son, Marvin P. Bush, is born.

1959—*Aug. 18:* His daughter, Dorothy W. "Doro" Bush, is born.

1964—*Nov. 3:* Fails in his bid to be elected to the Senate from Texas.

1966—*Nov. 8:* Elected to the U.S. House of Representatives from a Houston, Texas, district.

1970—*Nov. 5:* Loses another bid to be elected to the Senate.

—*Dec. 11:* Appointed U.S. ambassador to the United Nations.

1973—Becomes chairman of the Republican National Committee.

1974—Named head of the U.S. Liaison Office in China.

1976—Appointed director of the Central Intelligence Agency.

1980—*Nov. 4:* Elected vice president under Ronald Reagan.

1988—*Nov. 8:* Elected president of the United States.

1991—*Jan. 12:* Congress authorizes Bush to begin Persian Gulf War.

1992—*Nov. 5:* Loses presidential election to Bill Clinton.

1994—His son, George W. Bush, is elected governor of Texas.

1998—His son, Jeb, is elected governor of Florida.

2000—His son, George W. Bush, elected president of the United States.

2003—Travels and gives speeches on world affairs.

War in the Gulf, 1990–1991

On New Year's Eve 1990, President George H. W. Bush wrote a letter to his five children. They were all grown adults, and between the heavy demands of his own job and their busy lives, he did not get to see them much.

The president, though, was about to send young American soldiers to war, something that was hard for him to do. So hard, in fact, that talking about it could bring him to tears. So he wanted his five kids—George,

▲ Operation Desert Shield, beginning on August 7, 1990, was the buildup of American military units in Saudi Arabia in preparation for the war against Iraq. In November, President George Bush visited troops there. Here, he rides with General H. Norman Schwarzkopf.

Jeb, Neil, Marvin, and Dorothy—to know why he was doing it.

▶ Oily Problems

Earlier that year, the president of Iraq, Saddam Hussein, had accused a neighboring nation, Kuwait, of taking oil from his country's property. Oil is a valuable commodity, and Hussein threatened to use his army to get the oil back.

Iraq, which had 18 million people at the time, is the size of California. Kuwait was much smaller, with a population of just over two million. So when Iraq invaded Kuwait on August 2, 1990, it did not take long for Hussein's troops to overrun the country.

Now the problem facing Bush was how to ensure that Iraqi forces, which were just a few miles away from Saudi Arabia's important oil fields, did not enter that country too. If they had, Hussein would have controlled almost 40 percent of the world's oil supplies.

That was not something the United States was about to let happen.

Plus, another issue was nagging at the president's mind. Hussein was known to be a ruthless dictator, someone who rules by striking fear into his opponents, and sometimes even killing them. In a war with Iran during the 1980s, Hussein had used deadly chemical weapons.

In Bush's eyes, Saddam Hussein was a dangerous man, a killer. During Adolf Hitler's reign of power in Germany during the 1930s and 1940s, the world slowly learned how dangerous it can be when no country stops an international villain from taking over other countries. During the Holocaust, Hitler was responsible for the deaths of millions of Jews.

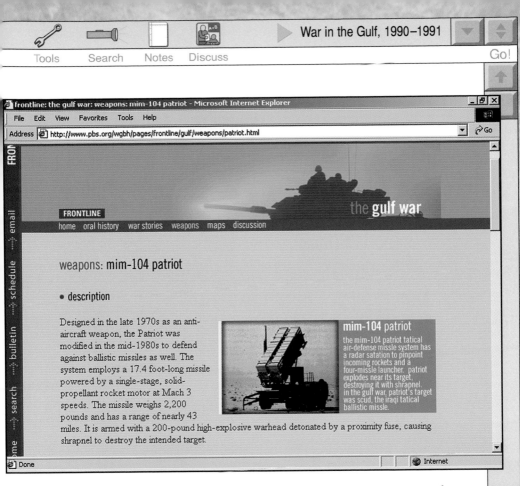

frontline: the gulf war: weapons: mim-104 patriot - Microsoft Internet Explorer

File   Edit   View   Favorites   Tools   Help

Address http://www.pbs.org/wgbh/pages/frontline/gulf/weapons/patriot.html

FRONTLINE

home   oral history   war stories   weapons   maps   discussion

weapons: mim-104 patriot

• description

Designed in the late 1970s as an anti-aircraft weapon, the Patriot was modified in the mid-1980s to defend against ballistic missiles as well. The system employs a 17.4 foot-long missile powered by a single-stage, solid-propellant rocket motor at Mach 3 speeds. The missile weighs 2,200 pounds and has a range of nearly 43 miles. It is armed with a 200-pound high-explosive warhead detonated by a proximity fuse, causing shrapnel to destroy the intended target.

mim-104 patriot

the mim-104 patriot tatical air-defense missile system has a radar satation to pinpoint incoming rockets and a four-missile launcher. patriot explodes near its target, destroying it with shrapnel. in the gulf war, patriot's target was scud, the iraqi tatical ballistic missle.

The Patriot missile system was one of the most important weapons of the Persian Gulf War. The Patriot was capable of shooting Iraqi Scud missiles out of the sky.

Bush was not going to sit still and watch Saddam Hussein spread his power. "I look at today's crisis as 'good' vs. 'evil,'" the president wrote to his children. "Yes, it is that clear."[1]

A Stern Warning

After consulting with other world leaders on the telephone, President Bush declared, "This will not stand, this aggression against Kuwait."[2] He built an alliance, or group of countries, to stand up against Iraq. The United States, Great Britain, and some other countries supplied soldiers.

Other countries contributed only money. All had the same goal in mind: to liberate Kuwait from Iraqi occupation. Eventually, more than forty nations contributed in some way by giving billions of dollars in aid, supplying logistical support, or sending troops. In all, the coalition included about 425,000 United States ground troops and 118,000 allied soldiers to face Hussein's million-man army.

With that support, the United States took its case to the United Nations (UN), an organization of most of

▲ On February 26, 1996, President Bush met with Kuwaiti leader Emir Shiek Amed Jaber Al-Sabah. They shared a private lunch to mark the fifth anniversary of the expulsion of the Iraqi army from Kuwait.

the world's countries. The UN's goal is to prevent war by finding peaceful solutions to world issues. On November 29, 1990, the UN passed a resolution telling Iraq it had until January 15, 1991, to leave Kuwait.

That deadline came, yet the Iraqi troops stayed. The next day, President Bush ordered bombing raids. The start of military action was known as Operation Desert Storm.

The Hundred-Hour War

The air and missile bombardment lasted six weeks. On February 24, American troops led a ground attack against the Iraqi positions in Kuwait. It must have been like using an umbrella to stop a flood. The ground war that forced Iraq out of Kuwait only lasted about one hundred hours.

President Bush ordered a halt to the war on February 27, saying that the United Nations mandate to drive Iraq out of Kuwait had been fulfilled. He decided against raiding Iraq's capital city, Baghdad, where Hussein remained in power.

Because the war was quick and successful and the United States did not suffer many casualties, a poll showed the president's approval rating had soared to 89 percent. As a result, many big-name Democrats dropped out of the 1992 presidential campaign, thinking they could never defeat such a popular president.

Yet the peace was not as easy to win as the war. Critics charged that the allied forces had stopped too soon, that the troops should have invaded Iraq and toppled Hussein. Others said such a move would have broken up the American-led coalition, causing arguments and chaos amongst otherwise friendly nations. They also said that trying to capture or kill Hussein and overthrow his government would have cost many more lives and would have put the allied forces in a position of having to rebuild Iraq. This would be very expensive.

Despite the disagreement from both points of view, Bush did say that the victory "licked the Vietnam syndrome"—meaning that the United States was not afraid to use military power for fear of a stalemate.[3]

The Kurds, an ethnic minority in northern Iraq, and Shiite Muslims in the south used Hussein's defeat to try and break away. Hussein used his army to crush the revolts. That caused the United States to establish "no-fly zones" in the north and south. The purpose of the aircraft-free zones was to prevent Iraq from using air power against the rebels.

Over the next decade, problems lingered in the Middle East. President Bush, who had led one of the quickest, cleanest military campaigns ever, eventually lost the White House to Bill Clinton. Saddam Hussein remained in power and was still running Iraq when Bush's son, George W., became president.

That led to a second showdown between a ruthless dictator and one of the most powerful families in American history.

Early Life, 1924–1941

George Bush was the type of friend every kid wanted to have. Polite and helpful, George's friends and family nicknamed him "Have Half" because he was always offering to share whatever he had with his siblings and his pals.

He was considerate, too. When he saw one of his high school classmates—a Jewish boy—being picked on, George ordered the bullies, "Leave the kid alone!"[1] The teasing stopped. Forty years later, that boy became a successful businessman named Bruce Gelb, and he helped Bush raise nearly $3 million to run for president.

Born on June 12, 1924, George Herbert Walker was the second child of Prescott and Dorothy Walker Bush. He had an older brother, Prescott (called "Pres"), and three younger siblings: Nancy, Jonathan,

George Bush was born in ▶ Milton, Massachusetts, on June 12, 1924.

and William (nicknamed "Bucky"). George was born in Milton, Massachusetts, but the family moved to Greenwich, Connecticut, while he was still a baby.

Though George had a few nicknames ("Fatty McGee McGaw" was one because he was a chubby toddler), only one stayed with him: He had been named after his maternal grandfather, George Herbert Walker, who was called "Pop." Therefore, George became "Poppy." Though he did not particularly like the nickname, it stuck for life.

A Family of Privilege

Money was never a problem for George's family. His father was an investment banker in nearby New York City, and his mother had grown up in one of St. Louis's richest families. "People say I was a man of privilege and by that they mean money," Bush said. "But I was privileged in the question of values—a mother and father who were determined to help their kids be good people."[2]

As her son remembers, Dorothy Bush taught her children values such as honesty, kindness, following your conscience, never whining, never complaining, and giving credit to other people. She insisted that her kids stick to those values.

One day, George came home and said, "Mother, I scored three goals in soccer!" "Fine, George," she answered. "But how did the team do?"[3]

Though Dorothy was both loving and firm, George's father was the more intimidating of the two parents. If they had been bad, the Bush kids knew they were in for a tough—and sometimes painful—punishment when Dorothy threatened to tell their father. Once, when George was in sixth grade and Pres in seventh, they had paid a classmate's sister to misbehave. When Dorothy found out, she told Prescott, who made the boys walk two miles to the girl's home to apologize.

George's father, who would become a United States senator in the 1950s, was quite formal: Even at home, the boys were required to wear jackets and ties at the dinner table. The family had a chauffeur named Alec who drove George to school, and they also had a nanny (Agnes) and a housekeeper (Nina).

At Greenwich Country Day School, George was well liked by his classmates. A good athlete, he was a first base-man in baseball, running back in football, and a soccer and tennis player. George was patient with kids who did not share his athletic ability. During a barrel race on the school yard one day, a heavy boy got stuck. While other kids chuckled, George helped him out and stayed by his side.

▲ Bush was a skilled athlete. He played baseball, football, soccer, and tennis as a youth. The future president (seated front row, center) continued to play baseball and soccer during his days at Phillips Andover Academy.

▷ Summers in Maine

Every summer, the Bush family traveled north to their seventeen-acre family estate in Maine. Called "Walker's Point," the land had been purchased in 1919 by Dorothy's father and grandfather. The Bush kids were often joined by their cousins as they searched the beach for starfish and sea urchins. Pres and George enjoyed taking their grandfather's lobster boat, *Tomboy*, into the Atlantic Ocean for fishing. Dorothy organized treasure hunts for the children and taught them to play a card game called bridge.

Prescott and Dorothy wanted their children to get the best education possible. For high school they sent George to a college preparatory institution in Andover, Massachusetts, called Phillips Academy. There, he earned grades that were acceptable—but not great. George again played baseball and soccer. He also served as editor of the school newspaper and as senior class president.

During the Christmas holiday in 1941, George was attending a dance at the Round Hill Country Club in Greenwich, Connecticut. He spotted a tall, pretty girl named Barbara Pierce and asked a friend to introduce him to her. They met, talked, then danced. George was seventeen, and Barbara was sixteen. Several months later, Barbara traveled to Andover to attend George's senior prom. After the dance, he walked her to the house where she was staying and, to say good-bye, kissed her on the cheek.

▷ In Love

"I floated into my room," Barbara wrote in her autobiography, " and kept the poor girl I was rooming with awake all night while I made her listen to how Poppy Bush was the greatest living human on the face of the earth."[4]

Military Man to Congressman, 1942–1970

Bush had planned on enrolling at Yale University directly after his graduation from Phillips Academy in 1942. Then after Japan's sneak attack on the United States military base in Pearl Harbor, Hawaii, in December 1941, he decided to enlist in the Navy.

He did exactly that on June 12, 1942—his eighteenth birthday. The usually stern Prescott Bush was saddened to tears. Years later, George said it was the first time he had ever seen his father cry.

▲ While Bush (center) was in the Navy, he practiced bombing runs with his fellow pilots. He flew a single-engine torpedo bomber called the TBF Avenger.

By this time, George Bush and Barbara planned to be married. She was off to college, and he was off to flight school. They communicated through letters and the occasional visit while George earned his wings. In June 1943, Bush was "commissioned" at age eighteen, making him the youngest pilot in the entire Navy. His torpedo bomber was called the *TBF Avenger*. By early 1944, Lieutenant Bush was flying attack missions in the South Pacific. He was a good pilot who built up the confidence of his men.

▶ Shot Down by the Enemy

On September 2, 1944, Bush received orders to blast radio towers on an island called Chichi Jima. The Japanese fighters detected him and attacked. "Suddenly there was a jolt, as if a massive fist had crunched into the belly of the plane," Bush remembered. "Smoke poured into the cockpit, and I could see flames ripping across the crease of the wing, heading toward the fuel tanks."[1]

Despite his burning aircraft, Bush stayed on target, dropping the bombs as ordered. After fulfilling the mission, he swung his plane over the water and parachuted out. Bush landed in the water, and though the Japanese were coming to fish him out and take him as a prisoner, an American submarine found him first.

Bush got lucky, surviving the experience with only a gash to his forehead. The two crew members who were in the plane with him were never found. "My heart aches for the families of those two boys with me," Bush wrote the next day in a letter to his parents. ". . . All and all it is terribly discouraging and frankly it bothers me a good deal."[2]

▶ Yale-Bound

For the bravery he showed by completing his mission, Bush received the Distinguished Flying Cross. In December, he was sent back to the United States. Together again with Barbara, the two married in Rye, New York, on January 6, 1945. He finally enrolled at Yale University in New Haven, Connecticut, majoring in economics. Bush's studies were accelerated—he planned to graduate in two-and-a-half years instead of the usual four.

At Yale, Bush's grades were among the best in his class. He joined a secret society called Skull and Bones and played soccer and baseball. As captain in his senior year, Bush met baseball legend Babe Ruth in a pre-game ceremony. During their time at Yale, George and Barbara Bush had their first son, George W., in 1946.

Bush graduated from Yale in 1948. Instead of joining his father as an investment banker on Wall Street, he struck out on his own with a job in the

George Bush married Barbara ▶ Pierce on January 6, 1945, in Rye, New York.

oil business. The Bushes and two-year-old "Georgie" moved to the Texas town of Odessa.

"If I were a psychoanalyzer, I might conclude that I was trying to, not compete with my father, but do something on my own," Bush later recalled about the move that took him far from the New England he knew. "Moving from New Haven to Odessa just about the day I graduated was quite a shift in lifestyle."[3]

Growing Job, Growing Family

During the oil boom days that followed World War II, the work was hard but rewarding. There were three thousand wells being drilled in the area just in the summer of 1948. Bush's job as a salesman was to make sure that as many of those drillers as possible used his company's equipment. That meant a lot of traveling and time away from his family, but it also meant Bush was meeting a lot of people. As his children grew older, Bush put his people skills to work organizing community or school events.

The hard work paid off. In 1950, Bush quit his job and formed his own company. The idea was to buy mineral rights on land where people were drilling for oil. If the wells produced oil, then the value of the mineral rights on the land that Bush's company owned would increase and his company could then sell those rights at a profit. Business was good and eventually, in 1953, Bush and some partners formed a company to drill for oil. Every one of the wells they drilled hit oil. Their successful company was called Zapata Petroleum Corporation. Success followed success because in 1954 the men started another company, which was called Zapata Off-Shore Company. George Bush was its president and it set out to drill for oil in the Gulf of Mexico.

▷ Sadness at Home

Although business was good, tragedy struck the Bush household. In 1953, the Bush's three-year-old daughter, Robin, died after a short battle with a blood disease called leukemia. Despite the tragedy of losing a daughter, there were some happy times in 1953 because that year another son, John, was born. The boy, nicknamed Jeb, would grow up to be governor of Florida. The family picture was completed by 1959 after Neil, Marvin, and Dorothy were born.

In 1952, George Bush's father, Prescott Bush, was elected to the U.S. Senate from Connecticut. Although the younger Bush was a Republican in a state that usually

▲ George and Barbara Bush would eventually have four sons and two daughters. Tragically, Robin, the eldest daughter, passed away from leukemia in 1953 at the age of three.

voted for Democrats, his father's successful campaign stirred his own interest in politics. Now was the time to use his skills and put all that time on the road meeting people and organizing events to work. In 1964, Bush decided to seek public office himself. He ran against incumbent Senator Ralph Yarborough. Although he campaigned hard across the state and had the backing of his family, he lost the election.

The experience just made him want to try again. So he learned what lessons he could from the loss and launched a campaign for Congress from his new home near Houston in 1966. This time, Bush won. He served in Congress for four years, pushing for civil rights laws that would give African Americans the same freedoms as white people.

In 1970, at the suggestion of former president and fellow Texan Lyndon Johnson, Bush kicked off another Senate campaign. He lost a close race to Lloyd Bentsen. By choosing to leave Congress and give the Senate a second shot, Bush was taking a chance. Now, he did not have a job, but that would soon change. Even though he had lost two Senate races, George Bush was a rising star in national Republican politics.

Career in Politics, 1971–1988

For at least some time, Bush considered getting out of politics after his second Senate loss. President Richard Nixon had personally asked him to run, and he assured Bush that he would get a job in the administration if he lost.

Nixon had a few jobs in mind—from putting Bush in charge of the space program—to making him an assistant to the president. What Bush wanted, however, was to become the U.S. Ambassador to the United Nations. He got the job and held it for twenty-two months.

In late 1972, Nixon asked Bush to become chairman of the Republican National Committee. Following the president's wishes, Bush accepted the position. His main job was to coordinate and lead the Republican's national efforts to get their candidates elected. However, when evidence started surfacing that Nixon knew about a break-in at the Democratic national headquarters, Bush's top priority switched to defending the president.

President Richard Nixon ▶ appointed George Bush U.S. ambassador to the United Nations and then chairman of the Republican National Committee.

For most of his twenty months as chairman, Bush traveled the country, trying to line up support for Nixon during the Watergate investigation. When it became obvious that Nixon had broken the law by covering up information, Bush sent him an official letter on August 7, 1974, encouraging him to resign. "I firmly feel that resignation is best for this country, best for this president," Bush wrote. "I believe this view is held by most Republican leaders across the country."[1]

Two days after receiving that letter—among many similar suggestions—Nixon resigned.

▶ Gaining Influence

When Nixon resigned, Vice President Gerald R. Ford became president. Bush wanted to be appointed vice president, and most Republican leaders liked him for the job. Ford, though, picked Nelson Rockefeller, former governor of New York, and told Bush he could choose any ambassadorship in the world. Bush picked China, where he served as Chief U.S. Liaison for thirteen months.

At Ford's request, Bush took charge of the Central Intelligence Agency (CIA) in 1976. As the country's top spymaster, Bush was responsible for overseeing the agency that coordinated many of America's spying and covert operations around the world. When Bush arrived, the CIA was under investigation for possible wrongdoings. Under such stress, many of the staff members were unhappy and felt unappreciated. As director of Central Intelligence, Bush followed the wishes of Congress. He reformed the CIA by replacing most of the top-level officials and securing more high-tech spying equipment, such as satellites. He also made an effort to make his employees feel welcome by doing things such as riding the same elevator as everyone else, instead of taking the private car reserved for the director.

During his time with the CIA, Bush kept out of politics. He still hoped to run for office again one day . . . only this time, his goals were higher than ever before.

▷ Presidential Dreams

Ford lost the 1976 presidential election to Jimmy Carter. This meant that Bush had only a couple of months remaining with the CIA. In early 1977, George and Barbara Bush moved back to Houston. As he started considering his different options, the idea of running for president seemed like a good one—and realistic, too.

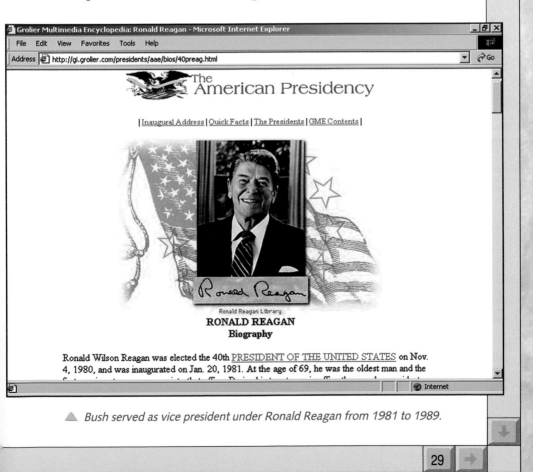

Grolier Multimedia Encyclopedia: Ronald Reagan - Microsoft Internet Explorer

File   Edit   View   Favorites   Tools   Help

Address   http://gi.grolier.com/presidents/aae/bios/40preag.html

The American Presidency

| Inaugural Address | Quick Facts | The Presidents | GME Contents |

Ronald Reagan Library

RONALD REAGAN
Biography

Ronald Wilson Reagan was elected the 40th PRESIDENT OF THE UNITED STATES on Nov. 4, 1980, and was inaugurated on Jan. 20, 1981. At the age of 69, he was the oldest man and the

▲ *Bush served as vice president under Ronald Reagan from 1981 to 1989.*

The series of jobs that Bush held during the 1970s prepared him well: Chairing the Republican National Committee gave him political power. His United Nations ambassadorship gave him great contacts around the world. Leading the CIA gave Bush a fine education on a wide range of worldwide issues.

Yes, running for president sounded like a good idea indeed. "Jimmy Carter had been elected," Bush said. "I went home to Texas and I started thinking, 'Well, why not?' I'd like to think I can help make things better, here and abroad."[2]

Bush spent nearly two years organizing his presidential campaign, and officially announced himself as a candidate in May 1979. His main competition for the Republican nomination was Ronald Reagan, a former movie actor and governor of California. After a series of hard-fought primary elections, Reagan won the nomination. Reagan then picked Bush to be his vice president. In November 1980, the Reagan-Bush ticket easily beat their Democratic opponents, President Jimmy Carter and Vice President Walter Mondale.

As Reagan's vice president from 1981 to 1989, Bush was extremely loyal to his boss, always supporting Reagan's view publicly even when he privately disagreed. "I'm for Mr. Reagan blindly," he once said.[3]

Vice President Bush traveled over one million miles during those eight years, representing the United States government at foreign leaders' funerals and in meetings between countries. He chaired task forces on drugs and terrorism, among other topics, and cast tie-breaking votes in the Senate to support President Reagan's plans to beef up America's military defenses.

Reagan and Bush in the ▶ White House.

After Reagan was wounded by a bullet in the spring of 1981, Vice President Bush ran the White House for two weeks while the president recovered. During Reagan's second term, Bush was suspected of guilt in the Iran-Contra Affair, in which members of the United States government had illegally traded weapons in return for the release of hostages. Bush proclaimed his innocence, and no one ever proved him guilty.

▶ Finally in the White House

After eight years in the White House, Ronald Reagan had reached his term limit. Now it was Bush's turn to run. He picked Dan Quayle, a senator from Indiana, as his running mate versus Democratic candidate Michael Dukakis and his vice presidential candidate, Lloyd Bentsen.

In a viciously negative campaign on both sides, Bush made a consistent promise to voters: "Read my lips," he would say. "No new taxes."[4]

It would be a promise Bush could not keep, but that—along with Reagan's popularity—helped Bush win the election, 54 percent to 46 percent. On November 1, 1988, twenty-two years after winning his first election, George Bush was poised to become president of the United States.

President Bush, 1989–1992

After taking the oath of office with his hand on the same Bible that George Washington had used nearly two hundred years earlier, George H. W. Bush became the forty-first president of the United States on January 20, 1989.

In his inaugural address, President Bush challenged the American people "to make kinder the face of the nation and gentler the face of the world."[1] To do that, he wanted better cooperation between government and non-profit organizations so that, working together, a "thousand points of light . . . spread like stars throughout the nation, doing good."[2]

The story of his time in office can be measured against those lofty goals and the struggle to achieve them. Some historians say that other than having a vague idea of where he wanted the country to go, Bush did not offer a specific agenda at the start of his term in office.

▶ The Push for Smaller Government

Although Bush had promised to spend more money on schools and create millions of more jobs, he did not want to raise taxes. In fact, he ran on that promise not to raise taxes, which he stated during his speech accepting the Republican presidential nomination: "The Congress will push me to raise taxes, and I'll say no. And they'll push, and I'll say no. And they'll push again, and I'll say to them, 'Read my lips. No new taxes.'"[3]

What Bush hoped was that private, community, and

nonprofit groups would help by taking over some of the burden of running some programs that the government funded. The first lady, Barbara Bush, got involved in domestic issues by taking on the cause of promoting literacy in the nation's schools. During her family's four years in the White House, she visited hundreds of schools and work sites of programs that encouraged people to read. She also founded the Barbara Bush Foundation for Family Literacy in 1989.

"I strongly believe that if every man, woman, and child in America could read, write and comprehend," she said, "we would be much closer to solving many of our nation's serious problems."[4]

American Memory Digital Item Display - 00652329 - Microsoft Internet Explorer

File   Edit   View   Favorites   Tools   Help

Address   http://memory.loc.gov/cgi-bin/query/i?ammem/pin:@field(NUMBER+@band(ppmsc+02869)):displayType   Go

Done   Internet

▲ George H. W. Bush was inaugurated as the forty-first president on January 20, 1989.

▶ The Cold War Melts

On the international scene, there was an easing of tensions (called the "Cold War") between the United States and the Soviet Union. The Soviet's new approach and attitude toward the West began in the last days of the Reagan administration. At home and abroad, the Soviet Union's economy floundered as the costs of the arms race continued to climb. After a series of personal meetings with Soviet leader Mikhail Gorbachev, the United States and Soviet governments agreed to cut back on the number of nuclear weapons.

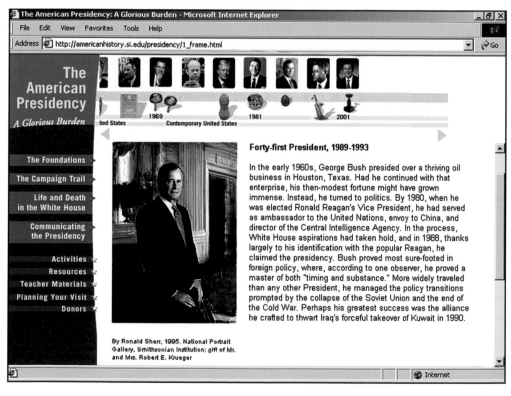

The American Presidency: A Glorious Burden - Microsoft Internet Explorer

File   Edit   View   Favorites   Tools   Help

Address http://americanhistory.si.edu/presidency/1_frame.html

The American Presidency
A Glorious Burden

1969   Contemporary United States   1981   2001

ited States

The Foundations
The Campaign Trail
Life and Death in the White House
Communicating the Presidency
Activities
Resources
Teacher Materials
Planning Your Visit
Donors

Forty-first President, 1989-1993

In the early 1960s, George Bush presided over a thriving oil business in Houston, Texas. Had he continued with that enterprise, his then-modest fortune might have grown immense. Instead, he turned to politics. By 1980, when he was elected Ronald Reagan's Vice President, he had served as ambassador to the United Nations, envoy to China, and director of the Central Intelligence Agency. In the process, White House aspirations had taken hold, and in 1988, thanks largely to his identification with the popular Reagan, he claimed the presidency. Bush proved most sure-footed in foreign policy, where, according to one observer, he proved a master of both "timing and substance." More widely traveled than any other President, he managed the policy transitions prompted by the collapse of the Soviet Union and the end of the Cold War. Perhaps his greatest success was the alliance he crafted to thwart Iraq's forceful takeover of Kuwait in 1990.

By Ronald Sherr, 1995. National Portrait Gallery, Smithsonian Institution; gift of Mr. and Mrs. Robert E. Krueger

Internet

▲ *During George Bush's administration, the United States became more involved in world affairs. One of his major accomplishments was helping to end the Cold War.*

The Cold War soon ended after the Berlin Wall that divided Germany into two countries came down in late 1989. By 1991, most of the countries that had made up the Soviet Union declared their independence.

The Cold War was over, and the personal relationship that Bush had built with Gorbachev throughout the 1980s helped make it happen. "I believed in Gorbachev," Bush said. "I believed in his word."[5]

Other Tensions Build

Yet Bush also faced challenges on this side of the world during his first year in office. Panamanian leader Manuel Noriega was beaten in the presidential race in May 1989, but he ignored the results of the election because a political rival won the presidency. Noriega was also suspected of involvement in the illegal drug trade and of laundering money for other drug lords. In response, Bush sent American troops to the United States base near the Panama Canal. Tensions and incidents mounted and, on December 20, American soldiers attacked Noriega's headquarters and military bases. Noriega escaped to the offices of the Vatican's representative in Panama but agreed to surrender to United States soldiers a little while later. He was found guilty of drug dealing in a Florida court and was sentenced to prison.

Undoubtedly, however, Bush's biggest challenge came when the Iraqi army invaded neighboring Kuwait in August 1990. The invasion and Iraqi occupation endangered oil production and supplies because the world got about 10 percent of its oil from Kuwait, a small country on the Persian Gulf. Hussein's bold move also threatened the stability of the region since Kuwait bordered oil-rich Saudi Arabia, a United States ally.

▲ President Bush shakes hands with troops stationed in Saudi Arabia in November 1990.

Bush drew on his long years of international service and his contacts to build a coalition of European and Middle Eastern nations against Hussein. The United Nations passed a resolution that would allow the United States and its allies to use force if Iraq did not leave Kuwait by January 15, 1991. Yet the diplomats could not persuade Hussein to withdraw his troops, and the United States started bombing targets in Iraq and occupied Kuwait on January 16, 1991. On February 24, American troops entered Kuwait. The ground war was over one hundred hours later.

"As Commander in Chief, I can report to you our armed forces fought with honor and valor. And as

President, I can report to the nation aggression is defeated. The war is over."[6]

However, even in victory, some were criticizing Bush for not pursuing Hussein's troops into Iraq and toppling Hussein from power. Bush replied that the original goal of the UN resolution was met: Iraqi troops had retreated and were no longer in Kuwait. Besides, he said, the coalition might not hold up if the war aims changed.

Because of victory in Operation Desert Storm, Bush's popularity rose to 89 percent, which was higher than any other president up to that point in time.

Falling From Grace

The government needed more money and Bush was forced to agree with Congress to raise taxes in 1990, something he had promised not to do. Over the following two years, his popularity steadily declined, mainly because the economy was lagging.

Up for reelection in 1992, Bush faced a difficult challenger. Arkansas Governor Bill Clinton was youthful (in his forties), a smooth speaker, and energetic. He performed well on television and appealed to a younger crowd of voters, one time even playing the saxophone during an appearance on a late-night talk show. Another candidate troubled Bush even more. Billionaire businessman H. Ross Perot launched a serious, well-financed bid for the presidency, targeting many of the same voters who would have supported the president.

During his time in the White House, Bush had closed out the Cold War, overthrown a drug-pushing dictator, and won the Persian Gulf War. Yet the American economy was in bad shape and Bush had broken one of his biggest promises: He raised taxes. That is what people

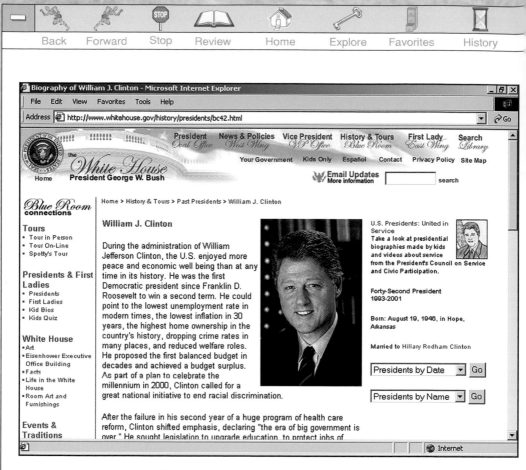

the White House

President George W. Bush

President · News & Policies · Vice President · History & Tours · First Lady · Search
Oval Office · West Wing · VP Office · Blue Room · East Wing · Library

Your Government   Kids Only   Español   Contact   Privacy Policy   Site Map

Email Updates
More information   search

Blue Room
connections

Home > History & Tours > Past Presidents > William J. Clinton

Tours
- Tour in Person
- Tour On-Line
- Spotty's Tour

Presidents & First Ladies
- Presidents
- First Ladies
- Kid Bios
- Kids Quiz

White House
- Art
- Eisenhower Executive Office Building
- Facts
- Life in the White House
- Room Art and Furnishings

Events & Traditions

William J. Clinton

During the administration of William Jefferson Clinton, the U.S. enjoyed more peace and economic well being than at any time in its history. He was the first Democratic president since Franklin D. Roosevelt to win a second term. He could point to the lowest unemployment rate in modern times, the lowest inflation in 30 years, the highest home ownership in the country's history, dropping crime rates in many places, and reduced welfare roles. He proposed the first balanced budget in decades and achieved a budget surplus. As part of a plan to celebrate the millennium in 2000, Clinton called for a great national initiative to end racial discrimination.

After the failure in his second year of a huge program of health care reform, Clinton shifted emphasis, declaring "the era of big government is over." He sought legislation to upgrade education, to protect jobs of

U.S. Presidents: United in Service
Take a look at presidential biographies made by kids and videos about service from the President's Council on Service and Civic Participation.

Forty-Second President
1993-2001

Born: August 19, 1946, in Hope, Arkansas

Married to Hillary Rodham Clinton

Presidents by Date ▾ Go

Presidents by Name ▾ Go

Internet

▲ *George Bush lost to Arkansas Governor Bill Clinton in the 1992 presidential election.*

remembered on Election Day in November 1992. Perot won a respectable 19 percent of the vote. Bush captured 38 percent, and Clinton won 43 percent.

Four years after gaining election to the most powerful job in the world, George H. W. Bush had been voted out.

Post Presidency,
1993 to Present

President Bush was sickened over losing the White House. He had led the nation through a successful war and conducted himself with integrity and grace. Losing to Bill Clinton bothered him deeply. The president's mother passed away only weeks after the election, which hurt even more.

Bush's final days as president in January 1993 were heart wrenching. After four years as president, eight as vice president, and many more before that as a public official, he was heartbroken to be leaving.

Soon after he and Barbara returned home to Houston, he started to feel better.

"It hurt a lot," he said, "But the minute we got back to Houston, Texas, and were welcomed by our neighbors, and went into that little house with two dogs and Barbara and me and nobody else, we began to say, 'Hey, life's pretty good.'"[1]

▶ Private Citizens—In a Way

The Bushes enjoyed their newfound freedom and privacy, though no former president or first lady are ever completely free to lead a private life. George and Barbara Bush began doing things they had not done for twelve years, ever since his election as vice president. For one, they went car shopping. Barbara was not sure if she would remember how to drive; it turns out that she did. She also began cooking their meals again. They also went shopping for

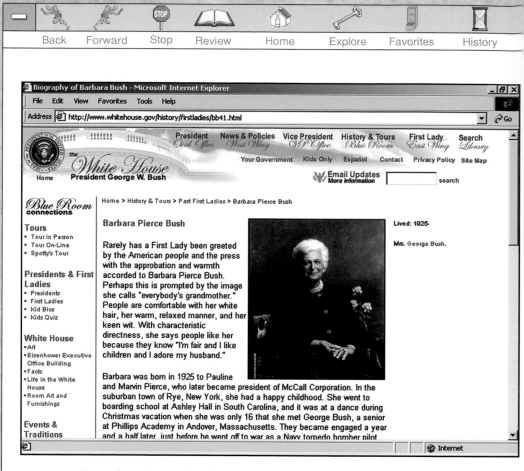

Back   Forward   Stop   Review   Home   Explore   Favorites   History

Biography of Barbara Bush - Microsoft Internet Explorer

File   Edit   View   Favorites   Tools   Help

Address   http://www.whitehouse.gov/history/firstladies/bb41.html   Go

President   News & Policies   Vice President   History & Tours   First Lady   Search
Oval Office   *West Wing*   *VP Office*   *Blue Room*   *East Wing*   *Library*

the
White House
President George W. Bush

Your Government   Kids Only   Español   Contact   Privacy Policy   Site Map

Email Updates
More information   search

Home

Blue Room
connections

Home > History & Tours > Past First Ladies > Barbara Pierce Bush

Tours
- Tour in Person
- Tour On-Line
- Spotty's Tour

Presidents & First Ladies
- Presidents
- First Ladies
- Kid Bios
- Kids Quiz

White House
- Art
- Eisenhower Executive Office Building
- Facts
- Life in the White House
- Room Art and Furnishings

Events & Traditions

Barbara Pierce Bush

Rarely has a First Lady been greeted by the American people and the press with the approbation and warmth accorded to Barbara Pierce Bush. Perhaps this is prompted by the image she calls "everybody's grandmother." People are comfortable with her white hair, her warm, relaxed manner, and her keen wit. With characteristic directness, she says people like her because they know "I'm fair and I like children and I adore my husband."

Barbara was born in 1925 to Pauline and Marvin Pierce, who later became president of McCall Corporation. In the suburban town of Rye, New York, she had a happy childhood. She went to boarding school at Ashley Hall in South Carolina, and it was at a dance during Christmas vacation when she was only 16 that she met George Bush, a senior at Phillips Academy in Andover, Massachusetts. They became engaged a year and a half later, just before he went off to war as a Navy torpedo bomber pilot

Lived: 1925-

Mrs. George Bush.

Internet

▲ *Barbara Bush's friendly and outgoing personality was an asset to her husband's political career. She continues to support many causes, including AIDS and homelessness, however, literacy has always been her main concern.*

groceries and other goods. A nearby Sam's Club quickly became their favorite store.

Of course, the Bushes could not do those things without attracting a big crowd of onlookers and autograph seekers. The same thing, however, happened in their front yard. Once, a busload of British tourists pulled up and wanted to chat and pose for pictures with the former President and Mrs. Bush. One of the Bush's neighbors politely shooed the vacationers away.

Realizing they would never become invisible in public, the Bushes at least wanted privacy at their home. They persuaded Texas lawmakers to approve a special regulation that allowed the Bushes and their neighbors to have a gate erected at the entrance of their horseshoe-shaped street.

Like most former first couples, the Bushes found that they enjoyed being able to choose what causes they wanted to support. Bush continued to work with the Points of Light Foundation, a volunteer group he founded while president in 1990. Barbara kept pushing reading through her Barbara Bush Foundation for Family Literacy.

Old Friends, Old Enemies

President Bush gave speeches around the world and kept in touch with many people he had met, hosting old friends at his homes in Houston and Kennebunkport, Maine.

He granted some interviews to the media and declined others, choosing the topics he

On April 13, 1993, two vehicles filled with explosives were driven to the outskirts of Kuwait City in a mission to assassinate former President George Bush. U.S. officials are almost certain that Iraqi President Saddam Hussein ordered the attack.

wanted to address. For example, when *Washington Post* reporter Bob Woodward wanted to talk to him about how the Watergate scandal affected every American presidency from Nixon through Clinton, Bush said no. "Out of office now," Bush wrote in a letter to Woodward, "away from Washington, out of national politics I have a freedom now that I treasure."[2]

Free as he was, Bush could not completely escape his past battles. In the spring of 1993, he visited Kuwait City to receive an award. Authorities there arrested sixteen men who had plans to kill Bush with a 175-pound car bomb. In June, an investigation by the United States government confirmed that the attack was ordered by Iraq, almost certainly at the command of President Saddam Hussein. Two of the men arrested were Iraqis.

Angered at the plot against his fellow president, Bill Clinton called Bush and told him, "It's clear it was directed against you. I've ordered a cruise-missile attack."[3]

Of course, that failed assassination plot would not be the final Bush versus Hussein fight.

▶ A Governing Family

By the late 1990s, as two of his sons became governors (George W. in Texas, Jeb in Florida), Bush carefully avoided making public comments about current issues. He did not want to overshadow his sons or mistakenly portray his opinions as theirs.

When George W. was elected as the forty-third president of the United States, that became even more important. The elder Bush chose to act only as father, not as a political adviser. While the son hired many of his father's former aides, the relationship between George and George W. remained strictly personal. The elder Bush cried in happiness during the weeks leading up to his son's inauguration in January 2001. They were only the second father-son combination to serve as president; the other was John Adams and his son, John Quincy Adams.

In tribute to that, Bush began referring to George W. as "Quincy." One day before his son's Saturday afternoon swearing-in ceremony, Bush told Republican leaders, "I'm going home Sunday, and leave this to Mr. Quincy."[4]

▶ The Bush Legacy

Many of the issues faced by Bush and his son are similar: Both dealt with a struggling economy. Each pushed for

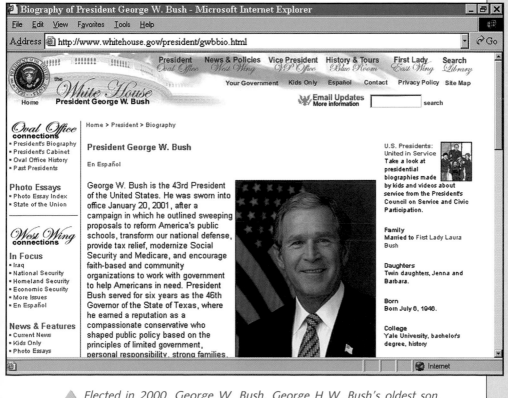

▲ Elected in 2000, George W. Bush, George H.W. Bush's oldest son, carries on the family legacy. They are the second father-son combination to serve as president of the United States.

improvements to the education system. Terrorism was an issue for the Bushes, though the September 11, 2001, attacks made it a much higher priority for George W. In 2003, a dozen years after Operation Desert Storm, George W. Bush hoped to do the one thing his father did not in dealing with Iraq: Capture or kill Saddam Hussein. His mission was called Operation Iraqi Freedom.

George H.W. Bush may not be remembered as one of the great American presidents. Yet, he is an important part of one of the most powerful families in United States history. In addition, his administration will be remembered for their foreign policy successes in Panama and Iraq. Former Secretary of State James Baker once said, "The president saw a chance to take on the two central problems of our age—the struggle for freedom and the threat of nuclear war—and he seized it. No apologies for that."[5]

When his son was elected over Al Gore, vice president to a popular but controversial Bill Clinton, it was a clear message: After eight years of scandalous allegations during the Clinton administration, Americans wanted to return a sense of dignity—maybe even royalty—to the White House. To do that, they chose a Bush.

That is exactly the way that George Herbert Walker Bush wants it. When asked how he wanted his presidency to be remembered, his answer was simple:

"He did his best. Did it with honor."[6]

Chapter 1. War in the Gulf, 1990–1991

1. George Bush, *All the Best: George Bush* (New York: Scribner, 1999), pp. 496–497.

2. Fred I. Greenstein, *The Presidential Difference: Leadership Style from FDR to Clinton* (Princeton, N.J.: Princeton University Press, 2000), p. 166.

3. Henry F. Graff, *Presidents: A Reference History*, Second Edition (New York: Macmillan Library Reference USA, 1997), p. 601.

Chapter 2. Early Life, 1924–1941

1. Bonnie Angelo, *First Mothers* (New York: HarperCollins Publishers, 2000), p. 351.

2. Philip B. Kunhardt, Jr., Philip B. Kunhardt III, and Peter W. Kunhardt, *The American President* (New York: Riverhead Books/Penguin Putnam, 1999), p. 337.

3. Angelo, p. 335.

4. Barbara Bush, *Barbara Bush: A Memoir* (New York: Lisa Drew Books/Scribner, 1994), p. 19.

Chapter 3. Military Man to Congressman, 1942–1970

1. Daniel Rubel, *Mr. President: The Human Side of America's Chief Executives* (Alexandria, Va.: Time-Life Books, 1998), p. 244.

2. George Bush, *All the Best: George Bush* (New York: Scribner, 1999), p. 51.

3. Bill Minutaglio, *First Son: George W. Bush and the Bush Family Dynasty* (New York: Three Rivers Press, 1999), p. 25.

Chapter 4. Career In Politics, 1971–1988

1. George Bush, *All the Best: George Bush* (New York: Scribner, 1999), p. 193

2. Philip B. Kunhardt, Jr., Philip B. Kunhardt III,and Peter W. Kunhardt, *The American President* (New York: Riverhead Books/Penguin Putnam, 1999), pp. 337–338.

3. Daniel Rubel, *Mr. President: The Human Side of America's Chief Executives* (Alexandria, Va.: Time-Life Books, 1998), p. 243.

4. George H. W. Bush, "Acceptance Speech," Republican National Convention, August 18, 1988.

Chapter 5. President Bush, 1989–1992

1. Henry F. Graff, *Presidents; A Reference History*, second edition. (New York: Macmillan Library Reference USA, 1997), p. 593.

2. Ibid.

3. Fred I. Greenstein, *The Presidential Difference: Leadership Style from FDR to Clinton* (Princeton, N.J.: Princeton University Press, 2000), p. 159.

4. Philip B. Kunhardt, Jr., Philip B. Kunhardt III, and Peter W. Kunhardt, *The American President* (New York: Riverhead Books/Penguin Putnam, 1999), pp. 337–338.

5. Daniel Rubel, *Mr. President: The Human Side of America's Chief Executives* (Alexandria, Va.: Time-Life Books, 1998), p. 338.

6. Greenstein, p. 159.

Chapter 6. Post Presidency, 1993 to Present

1. Philip B. Kunhardt, Jr., Philip B. Kunhardt III,and Peter W. Kunhardt, *The American President* (New York: Riverhead Books/Penguin Putnam, 1999), p. 339.

2. Bob Woodward, *Shadow: Five Presidents and the Legacy of Watergate* (New York: Simon & Schuster, 1999), p. 222.

3. George Stephanopoulos, *All Too Human* (New York: Little, Brown and Company, 1999), p. 162.

4. Frank Bruni, "Triumph for Father and Son, And a Wellspring of Feeling," *New York Times*, January 21, 2001, p. 13.

5. James Baker, as quoted in William A. DeGregorio, *The Complete Book of U.S. Presidents: From George Washington to Bill Clinton* (New York: Wings Books, 1997), p. 698.

6. Kunhardt et. al., p. 339.

Further Reading

Blanton, Tom, Barry Bluestone, Eugene Carroll, Jr., et. al. *Eyes on the President: History in Essays and Cartoons.* Santa Rosa, Calif.: Chronos Publishing, 1993.

Francis, Sandra. *George Bush: Our Forty-First President.* Chanhassen, Minn.: Child's World, Inc., 2001.

Holden, Henry M. *The Persian Gulf War.* Berkeley Heights, N.J.: MyReportLinks.com Books, 2003.

Joseph, Paul. *George Bush.* Edina, Minn.: ABDO Publishing Company, 1999.

Lucas, Eileen. *Reagan, Bush, and Clinton.* Vero Beach, Fla.: Rourke Corporation, 1996.

Nardo, Don. *The War Against Iraq.* Farmington Hills, Mich.: Gale Group, 2001.

Pemberton, William E. *George Bush.* Vero Beach, Fla.: Rourke Corporation, 1993.

Schuman, Michael A. *George H. W. Bush.* Berkeley Heights, N.J.: Enslow Publishers, Inc., 2002.

Stefoff, Rebecca. *George H. W. Bush: Forty First President of the United States.* Ada, Okla.: Garrett Educational Corporation, 1992.

Strait, Sandy. *What Was It Like In Desert Storm?* Unionville, N.Y.: Royal Fireworks Publishing Company, 2001.

		STOP					
Back	Forward	Stop	Review	Home	Explore	Favorites	History

Index